Equinox

A Gathering of T'ang Poets

Equinox

Translations and adaptations

by DAVID GORDON

Ohio University Press

Library of Congress Catalog Card Number: 73-181682
ISBN 8214-0162-9 181682
Manufactured in the United States of America
by the Watkins Printing Company
Design by Harold M. Stevens

ACKNOWLEDGEMENTS
Some of these poems first appeared in the following publications: *Concerning Poetry,
Arx, Tentacle, Monument, College English, Hierophant, New England Review, Seneca Review, Northeast, Yes, Poet Lore, Maine Times,* and *Literature East and West* (The University
of Texas at Austin).

For Ellen

Contents

Introduction

Man as part of nature is a theme repeated by poets from the T'ang and Sung dynasties. Man's world seen from the perspective of the world of nature produces much of the sense of toleration, serenity, wholeness and the breadth of humanitarian ideals that we find in these poems.

Ignazio Paz has described a great difference between eastern and western cultures in terms of a culture's balancing of the body v. the non-body, or the mind v. matter.[1] He has found that in western cultures generally the balance between these is often quite precarious and in China by contrast, there has generally been an unusually fine balancing between body and non-body. What this comes to in human terms is the degree of toleration and understanding man extends to what his body means symbolically.

In the west the body represents the inferior part of himself, and by extension, the world of nature, the female, and races other than his own. In many western cultures since the seventeenth century, man's relationship with nature had assumed the ominous antagonism of Dr. Jekyll v.Mr. Hyde, a relationship in which nature was to be feared, and therefore hated and by consequence destroyed. (Perhaps we are beginning to reap the ecological harvest of this kind of thinking.) In the China of these poems on the other hand, man appears to be at home in nature; he is unseparated from it, whereas in the west there appears to be a long record of cultural schizophrenia that has kept man warring against what may be his better half. Perhaps China of the T'ang and Sung dynasties serves as a good example of a country that had not suffered the effect of

---

[1] Ignazio Paz, "The Revolt of the Body," *Hudson Review,* XXIII, No. 4 (Winter 1970-71), 658.

Introduction

"disassociation of sensibility," as T. S. Eliot has described what happened to English poetry and culture after the seventeenth century.

In order to appreciate Chinese art one must understand all of Chinese thought, not just one part of it. Toleration goes to the heart of their poetry, art and philosophy (Confucius was relatively free from prejudice[2]). A toleration that we can discern in the early Chinese bronzes.

For example, a typical *chüeh* cup of the Shang dynasty will have a design that is made up of parts of several animals, or a design of a dragon will itself be constructed out of a number of small dragon figures. Even at this early time a sense of inclusiveness of separate parts into a meaningful unity can be seen.

Another typical *ku* ritual drinking vessel will have a design of an ox made up of dragons, a cicada, snakes, thunder and cloud patterns. Here we see how all the parts going to form the whole, an important food animal, are themselves symbols of important agricultural functions; the dragon and snake, are rain symbols, and the cicada sings as the summer is maturing the crops, all making up a unity that is not dominated by man, as Achille's shield is, but simply implying the quite unassuming and *dependent* presence of man.

We might ask if there is anything unusual about the representation of man simply helping himself to a slice of nature. Perhaps the unusual thing is in the way the Chinese represent it. The *being-in* the same ecology that feeds him is paleolithic, as Alexander Marshack has shown us in stone age art where animals are used as characters in stories explaining human processes. The understanding of the seasonal rhythms of paleolithic life is the most important wisdom man can attain if he is going to survive.[3]

---

[2] cf. James Legge, trans., *The Chinese Classics; Confucian Analect* (Hong Kong; Hong Kong Univ. Press, 1960), 1, Bk. ix, Ch. iv, 217.

[3] Alexander Marschack, *The Roots of Civilization: The Cognitive Beginnings of Man's First Art, Symbol and Notation* (N.Y.: McGraw-Hill, 1973), p. 316 ff. 372 ff.

Introduction

This sense of wholeness is a pervasive theme throughout the early bronzes, and as the modern Chinese philosopher Chang Tung-sun has said, "The concept of all things forming one body has been a persistent tendency in Chinese thought from the beginning until now."[4]

The Chinese have always thought in terms of things getting along side by side, forming some kind of a pattern; in such coordinate thinking, concepts are allowed to retain their identity and are not subsumed beneath one another. This kind of correlative thinking sees all the correspondences in nature forming one huge pattern. We may ask if this doesn't smack of magic and the supernatural. Magic, yes. But a kind of magic that modern science is beginning to recognize as the most valid way of describing the world we live in. But rather than call it supernatural, the "Organicism" of Alfred North Whitehead would be more fitting.

Musical harmony has been native to the Chinese way of considering man's place in nature, a non-mechanical, spontaneous order in which all things, including man, fulfill themselves as musicians in an orchestra cooperating in one unified music.

The idea of an order that goes by itself has appeared in many different guises, from early Chinese philosophy, in which the unity of the universe is definitely stated, down to the present day. Whereas some philosophies try to describe the universe as if they were taking sides between warring ideologies, such as mind v. matter, Chinese thought has traditionally accepted the polar opposites in nature as necessary for mutual existence. For example, the legendary archetypal culture hero, Shun, was said to exhibit exemplary illumination because he could listen to opposing views on any matter and thereby determine what was correct by conciliating opposites into a unity. Each one of the poets included here tells us,

---

[4] Chang Tung-sun, " A Chinese Philosopher's Theory of Knowledge," *Yenching Journal of Social Studies*, 1 (1939) 155.

among other things, something about his experience with unity as a way, *tao*.

Lao Tzu tells us that the *Tao* is the most inclusive of all principles in the universe, and with this as a start, he laid the foundation for one of the most important schools of thought in China, at about the same time as Confucius, and rivalling Confucianism in significance.[5]

The *tao* is both a mystical and transcendental principle as well as an experiential and practical principle of everyday life. In fact, as the way of the natural and spontaneous, its simplicity, tranquility, non-active participation, and emphasis on contemplative intelligence make it the complimenting opposite of the orderliness, agressiveness, active participation, and emphasis on practical intelligence of Confucianism.

It is useful to parallel these two important philosophies of China with one of the very earliest classics, the *Yi Ching (Book of Changes)*, which draws a cosmological representation of the world in terms of the interplay of two cosmic sexual forces, the Yin and Yang. Yin, the female element is associated with qualities such as yielding, earth, night, moon, intuitive mystical intelligence and (for the purposes of the parallel) Taoism. Yang, the male element, is associated with assertiveness, sunlight, air, dominating rational intelligence, and Confucianism. (We may recall the daylight world of consciousness of James Joyce's *Ulysses* as contrasted with the nighttime dream world of the unconscious of his *Finnegann's Wake*.) The universe is seen as an interaction of these two natural forces, a state of continuous change.

By means of a superlative poetic language that uses 64 hexagrams, all possible forms of change within the universe can be expressed and accounted for; a non-static, systematic and natural philosophy that has functioned in the harmonious development of Chinese society, ethics and civilization.

The Book of Changes is of interest to us because it became the

---

[5] cf. Lin Lutang, *The Wisdom of Lao Tzu*, (N.Y.: Random House, 1948), p. 51

Introduction

Confucian classic that formed the common bond of kinship with the Taoist school. Confucians and Taoists found in it a satisfactory moral, political, scientific and cosmological explanation of the universe.

What is of considerable importance for these T'ang and Sung poets is that they were experiencing the beginning of a synthesis between the Confucian and Taoist schools, and it would not do them justice to try to sharply divide them into either one school or the other.

Since the entire development of Chinese thought seems to have always been toward a profounder realization of unity, it is only by carefully understanding some of the apparent differences that we can come to appreciate something of the composite effect made up of these two opposites, as a third factor, Buddhism, entered.

Another Confucian classic, *The Doctrine of the Mean, the Chung Yung,* was very important to the Taoists because it discusses how human nature is actually joined with cosmic equilibrium and harmony. It describes how man and nature form a unity in terms that are at once psychological, metaphysical and extremely practical in everyday life. Because of the far reaching mysticism of the *Chung Yung* it made a strong appeal to Buddhists as well as Taoists, and this in turn began to prepare the way for the influence Buddhism would exert on Confucianism in the synthesis that would now include all three of China's schools of thought, Confucianism, Taoism, and Buddhism.

And what was the significance of the way, *tao*, to these poets? We must remember that statesman or mystic, Confucian ruler or Taoist hermit, the Chinese always want a philosophy that is functional, that gets results. The *tao* originally meant a way of doing something. Confucius speaks of the *tao* of government, and he means a way that will work. Although the Taoists raised it to a transcendental principle of the universe, it never lost its very finite practical connotation of defining man's place in nature.

Introduction

Nature accepts man; man accepts nature, or as Seneca said, "If you're O.K., I'm O.K." "Si vales bene est, ego valeo." This relationship is similar to a type of thought we find in some western mystics, in which there is a connection with nature that is not based on fear, and thus on separation and hostility. Instead, it is based on affection and understanding.

It might be likened to the way a swimmer feels about the water when he has learned to float. There is a very delicate relationship, which would be destroyed by fear, in which he makes a pact with the law of bouyant objects.

These poets understand the *tao* as a gestalt discipline of the whole human organism similar to the discipline required in learning how to ride a horse, to ski, to canoe or to fly an airplane. On another level they understand it as the spiritual discipline involved in mystical contemplation, for example as the 12th century Richard of St. Victor describes in his *Benjamin Minor*. These Chinese poets understand the *tao* as a principle underlying both kinds of activities.

One doesn't swim by simply kicking his legs and flailing his arms. Swimming is an activity in which mind and body are unified. One's body and mind come to an understanding of the nature of water. In executing a stall or spin in a light plane one's whole body communicates sensations of weightlessness to the mind. We surrender our individual will in order to understand something of the way of the cosmos. If not, the canoe capsizes in the rapids. If it is not a surrender of will that is complete and confident, a horse can detect our fear, or the skis will not follow the curvature of the mountain slope.

Such ways of experiencing nature may serve as a rough pattern for a higher type of contemplation. Regardless of individual philosophical leanings, a broad cultural background was sufficiently available so that these poets would have had a more primordial understanding of nature than poets from a culture that was encumbered with superstitions, bigotry and fear.

Introduction

Thus for Confucian, Buddhist and Taoist alike, a broader philosophical toleration was possible in their view of the world. We may consider the *tao* as a modality of man's interaction with the non-human world, raised according to the degree of concentration and intensity, to a synthesis and fusion in which an alteration and heightening of awareness may take place. The non-human and human elements are brought for a moment into a harmonious relationship.

The world of nature as the home of humanity is not merely decorative detail in these poems, it is the grammar of a way of life.

In the study of this period I am indebted in particular to A. C. Graham, James Liu, Ch'en Shou-yi and Liu Wu-chi.

Some Notes on the Translations and Adaptations

I have tried to realize an ideogram specifically and in terms of its context especially when the *T'zu Hai*, Chang Hsüan and Bernard Kalgren are certain about its meaning and etymology; and certainly the richness of the language's multiple ambiguities (bluer than Ruskin's gentian) can help project an equivalent. I have condensed, expanded, abridged, used compression, ellipsis, inversion, impressionism and expressionism in an effort to directly translate the spirit of these poems (a literal translation is a pound of flesh without a drop of blood). (A few Sung poems are included which link the spirit of T'ang with the next dynasty).

Some examples:
'Night at Cloud Gate Hall' *by Sun T'i*

yen	hua	hsiang	wai	yu
mist	flowers	shape	outside	dark

But 'hsiang' as Kalgren shows in a Yin bone drawing is an elephant with trunk and tusks. Thus, to describe the nature of mist among the flower beds, "Mist wreathes the parterres with elephant/teeth."

'Your Bad News' *by Yüan Chen*

ts'an	teng	wu	yen	ying	ch'uang	ch'uang
injure	lamp	not	flame	shadow	flickering	

'Ch'uang also means 'flag' and 'screen.' I wanted to fuse the sickness of the poet and his bad news that transforms the flickering flame into, "Maimed flame falls from its circle into a bleared/flag.

'All Day the Hills Around the Shrine' *by Liu Ts'ang*

yüeh	ming	yao	t'ing	yüan	ts'un	chen
moon	bright	long	hear	distant	village	washing stone

A group of concept rimes in this poem; you can see how to the observer these visual and auditory accretions interweave each other. Kalgren notes that the component for 'yüan' is a long robe, 'giwan, yüan.' "In the village someone pounds the moon's robe/on a washing stone."

'In Transit, Sobering' *by Li Chang-fu*

t'ian   t'iao   t'ing lou   chung
remote remote hear drip all

'Lou' means 'drip,' but also 'a bronze pan to catch water, leak, flow through an opening, pierce, penetrate, loss, weak spot, run to waste banish, lose track of, secluded corner, clepsydra.' The sobering in a frontier village on a rainy morning, with its irregular rain drop beat, pervades the entire poem and ought to be rendered in its effect on the observer's own head, sunrise, trees, birds, air, flowers, his memory, leaked away time and finally his horse.

'Spring Dark' *by Wang An-shih*

yüeh i   hua   ying   shang lan   kan
moon moves flower shadow up   railing shaft

But the intensity of this observation is concentrated in the dominant figure of the moon and its motile effect on the flower which becomes the gesture of spring. 'I', however, also means 'migrate' as in the binom 'i wang.' And 'i' has the more basic meaning of 'change' (dia, i.e.) suitable for the moon. Note also the Greek origin of migrate, ἀμείβω, 'I change.' Thus, "A calyx of shadow/further up the railing's shaft/migrates to the moon."

'Wang Sun Driven to Hiding' *by Wang Wei*

wang sun   kuei   pu   kuei
king's grandson return not return

But reading the meaning of Wang Sun's flight from An Lu-shan's soldiers into this, we see that 'sun' also means 'prudent, go into hiding, to conceal.' Kalgren gives a Yin bone depicting a 'child and silk.' Thus the sense of fate concealing itself in his shirt as he is himself hiding out from the soldiers, is reinforced in the implication, "And fate lines your shirt's hem if you return."

Some Notes on the Translations and Adaptations

'Opposite Spring of Night' *by Ch'en Tzu-ang*
ch'ang ho   mo   hsiao t'ien
long   river   not   light   sky

Almost a *Romeo and Juliet* play on light, 'ch'ang ho' also means
the Milky Way. 'Mo' also means drowned, and in the binom
'mo ju,' to confiscate. 'Hsiao' further means dawn. Thus to
coalesce the visual impact of dawn and starlight pulling apart
as his moment of departure:

> Drowned star stream
> > confiscating
> > > dawn.

t'zu hui   tsai ho   nien
this meeting on   what year

But 'hui' also means 'happen, cover, calculate, keep together;'
and as Kalgren represents in a Chou III-IV inscription, what
is in fact a vessel with handles, covered by a lid (g'wâd, ywâi).
'Nien' primarily meant harvest, but also 'year.' Thus a vessel to
receive the emotional distillation;

> to leave
> time closed in a jar
> return in what autumn?

'Pear Blossoms' *by Su Shih*
meng = 'a fine penetrating drizzling rain' but in keeping with
the clusters of minute, hard, bony cells in the flesh of *Pyrus
Spectabilis,* "Grit-celled rainfall."

'Down North Ku Mountain' *by Wang Wan*
hai jih   sheng ts'an   yeh
sea sun   grows injuring night

I wanted to combine the sense of growth with the opposite and
definitely destructive sense of 'ts'an.' The usual paraphrase is,
'the waning night' or 'expiring night' but this weakens some-
what the coordinated action and I wanted to carefully balance
the two necessary forces as important movement in the whole
poem. "The sea sun is edging upwards/through the flaking
away night."

Some Notes on the Translations and Adaptations

'At Black Mountain' *by Chang Chiu-ling*
shai   lo   ch'u   chung yün
sprinkle fall comes heavy cloud
'Shai' has in its graph, as Kalgren notes, a drawing of a deer with a 'pair of fine horn (lieg, liei).' Thus, "A cloud of spray escalades/a gigantic rack of antlers."
'War Wall South' *by Li Po*
yeh   chan   ke   tou   szu
field battle resist quarrel kill
The *K'ang Hsi Tu Tien* notes a drawing of a sacrificial wine vessel as the component for 'tou,' (note labyrinthine image). 'Ke' also means 'exhaust,' 'reach the utmost point and obstruct (g'lăk); from Kalgren. Li Po is depicting a field, 'yeh,' from which there is no escape:

> a battlefield locks our lives in a labyrinth
> of unclocked combat
> and the wine is blood.

pai   ma   hao   ming hsiang t'ien   pei
destroy horse screams cries toward heaven laments
'Ming' and 'pei' are both precise words for the reflection on the tragic action that the horse renders to the sky for all the dead men, "A stabbed horse screams/a contralto's aria."

Equinox

At Anchor Beneath The Bridge

The moon, ruined, falls
into a crow's cry that fixes
the frost. The Liquidambar leaves
along shore, and the crouched embers
of fishermen's fires overlay
my sleep. Then the bell from Cold
Mountain Shrine at Ku Su
brings midnight aboard.

Chang Chi

At Black Mountain The Water Unrolls

Down the abyss the red water falls
through purple vapour looming up half way;
and from the sweep downward of whole hurled trees
a cloud of spray escalades
a gigantic rack of antlers;
and a rainbow domes the sun-wet air
in earshot of wind and rain;
as from the color of grain in head;
in the generating egg of mist
the mountain is conceived.

Chang Chiu-ling

Touched Is Met

Wild goose winging in high off the sea
won't turn aside at the reservoir ponds,
and paired kingfishers light in the pearled Chu tree,
cliff-high to outrange a bullet's reach.
Elegant clothes cramp the heart's touch; and high
thoughts bottle you in some sacred hate.
I go plain, pulled-down, unseen.
An arrow? At what would I aim?

Chang Chiu-ling

Wind On Tung T'ing

Long flat plain of river shadow
and all day wheeze of reedy grass
ring my anchored boat; zizania's
club shaped heads of grain by my
fishing line, its three month spikes
roll on smooth waves where willow catkins
pelt a ribband of mist. But
nothing lifts this dead weight of spring;
and I haven't a cent for wine.
Along the shore houses add up fishermen's
families, and on one side
the village sulks into evening.

Chang Pi

Nan Chung Inn Before Rain

Whine. Again crying as of children;
monkeys. And wild geese.
To roll up a window curtain and face
no answer.
Years float in bits; how many guest
years travelling from south Chu
to bring someone on his way, cuts
me off, the steepness. No home mail
survives these canonized frontiers;
and cleaving wind from the north
mounts stair steps
in the rain's swift fore.

Chang-sun Tso-fu

The Lake, Eighth Month

Eighth month water of Tungt'ing holds
lambent haze vesicles; Hsiao and
Hsiang Rivers both flowing northward.
We navigate a thousand
miles of dream-tide homewards
but wake in the dark fifth
watch before dawn to find in our
hands the same anchorless yaw.
My book satchel is a barred door,
but a wineshop sidetracks me
to meet the thought of old friends
all otherwhere, that we might
together again
knock around. . . .

Chang Wei

8

At Anchor, Sunfall

Lying on Huai roadstead
as frost braids false hair
in the night tide's aggressions,
a moon coasts the town walls,
a wafer of sand bivouacks
beneath geese and the market place twitters
with chickens. Those clouds and my
home state are aliens; but how to tie down
the self sown thought that travels the backbone?

Ch'ang Chien

As Chiu Hua A Spring

Nephrite towering into carved air,
to see it, leave Red Hill and unclose
your eyes. Where streams from the crag
converged on the sun, an anvil of cloud,
cumulonimbus, was incasing its roof.
Stretching its thousand year legs a crane
danced on its tree; and on the bridge
arching a rainbow I met
a densiflora pine, who wryed his
brows like a rain god
and asked me to chat.

Ch'en Tzu-ang

10

The Opposite Spring Of Night

Flame's silver rim spits
a spiralling thread of smoke
as a wine cup sits the open work mat.
              Tomorrow
from you, my leaving
goes through the strings' grave
guitars of my fingers' thoughts;
nothing by itself plays:
all the detours that will
harl me in a mountain gulch. Now
the moon's latencies tie
the lateward night in a tree's arms.
Drowned star stream
        confiscating
              dawn,
Lo Yang's road
broods at my feet
to leave
time closed in a jar
return in what autumn?

Ch'en Tzu-ang

Hwai South

From the south heading north,
to catch your breath here, there's time.
And autumn is already stale news when
you think the blown duckweed of Chu,
but it won't weigh you down
if at sunfall you listen to
the mountains themselves
give it tongue.

Ch'eng Hao

Its Bamboos

Gleaning months press
the small ground of years
around a man's feet.
But rose vapour,
the clouds and mists
merge in the shaws of Chu Monastery
and touch its ground.
Solicitude
to go back there
how many times
more?

Chu Fang

Staying Overnight On A Mountain Farm

Where grey-edged leaves
take down the sun
in the bamboos' aerial stems I spied
the gateway, a seat under the fasting moon.
A creek was distancing its stone bed;
an etherial rain contoured the west wind.
Then dawn razed the clouds. I
got up and untied my office seal;
and spring was already hilling toward the Massif of Nan.

Ch'u Kuang-hsi

14

Field's Family

Daylight wakes us to weed the fields;
then nightfall, we twist scutched hemp into thread.
Vigorous boys and girls energize
this farm; and teeny kids who can't weave
plant melon seeds in mulberry shade.

Fan Ch'eng-ta

Small Rain

Fine beads of rain
pave the road slick as cheese;
grass it seemed in the distance
but when I came near, no.
Within willow limbs spring
mist had insulated the town.

Han Yü

A Day's Other

Where I walked, some one, unknown
to me. The two of us sit like
old buddies taking in the idyllic
pines and pools. But he needn't feel so
broke not buying the wine. In my
pocket there's enough for us both.

Ho Chih-chang

Overnight On A Mountain

Plain toothed chestnut leaf
parquets its straight veined
layers with olive green.
Sepia twilighted bits of talk
along the upper stream bank. And the moon
grazing the old part of the hall's roof,
travelers turn in; but wind pushes the gate
ajar now and then for a not yet returned
monk.
    Night wet had webbed the mountain's husk
        as fireflies were threading the bamboos
back and forth over the water;
                  about midnight
I dozed off.
      Then the bell sound of dawn
was hustling me again into my clothes.

Hsiang Szu

Wei's Place On The Han

Knotting spear grass to thatch his own
roof, a cracked tortoise shell divined
the bedrock of his rammed-earth river home.
The homing sun flocks the birds
and he hears caulking mallets tap
night into seams between fishing boat
strakes.

Tide line raising the water to mark
trunks of along shore willows, the mountain
loans kingfisher woad to the kitchen's smoke.
Then Wei smiles the mulberry maund
to his wife's hand; spring close by,
how much longer can the silkworms sleep?

Jung Yü

Clear Easter

Slopes from the north and south
climb to a head above these tombs.
And Easter oscillates between sweeping
them clean and making the offerings; ash
of burned paper money somersaults upward
into white vanessa butterflies and spilt
tears bloody the azalea. Then
a fox naps on a grave mound in the tabling sun;
nightfall, children's laughter at the window
in the lamplight.
Now as long as life
grows inside you want to
pour some wine. Once you've arrived
below the nine earthen springs you
won't get
one
drop.

Kao Chü-ch'ing

20

Cashiered

He's not what you call mad;
you're just debarred
for awhile. I've in the past
walked that same road to Min Chung.
    In fall, geese, one or two come;
its only the apes at night, from the foothills,
their mourning, and eastward, clouds
join hands to box the road;
but southward the air, miasmal and foul.
A breakthrough you'll find; dew and rain.
Give a little with the waves and wind. But
don't give up.

Kao Shih

Toward The Frontier

Paired horses setting nightfall against
their hooves on a road that sinks into mire
no matter which way we detour;
the border came upon us in a man
wearing a large one piece cloak,
a locust's larval case. Here, streams
grind the unpeopled mountain downward through the unheard dried leaves.
No one spoke as we climbed to the pass,
and rain was curdling the air into snow.

Kao Shih

In Transit, Sobering

How far day persists in the wine-starred
rain, overhead dawns a waking into sleep,
a never unimposed receiving of single
drops haggard always against some roof's
frontier village above me. Rhapsodic
timing of an endless clepsydra;
soggy tree shadows have swollen
sunrise; and the month has waterlogged each
rhythm cast up between beats of rain.
The river road has jaded the birds,
and along the slope the wind has soused
new growings. Ten years gone, where? My
mangy horse has engorged the ruts
                              east and west.

Li Ch'ang-fu

War Wall South

Called the Shrivelled Mulberry Spring
Battle. Last year.
And then the one called the Tsung Shallows
Battle. This year.

(Distinctive sameness. Chronic; timeless.
Yorik kissing a chapless skull:
a perennial bloom from the human vacuum.)

"We'd done I figured. We dragged the armor
down to scour it in the breakers at T'iao.
And in the T'ien mountains that year we turned
loose the horses, snow clinging to grass bracts.
The great Wall Campaign, sick to get home
or what was left of it, had shrunk my veins.
And then they came down on us again,
Hsiung Huns
fertilizing their furrows with our folks' bones.

But beacons! And tamped walls with the antique names!
Beaconless home but this beacon never goes out.
A battlefield locks our lives in a labyrinth
of unclocked combat
and the wine is blood. A stabbed horse screams
a contralto's aria as a kite out of our eyes'
range beaks a closed man's eyes, flies,
impales a bite-sized man on a withered
stob. And in the absence of generals

24

the essence of officers and men slubbers the grass.

Because this intricate dish of murder
                    is.

    Li Po

It Was Autumn

A branch of the Hsiang River skeins
silk on the moon's reel as an egret
lobs the white up with its wings.
A man hears a girl picking chestnuts
by the shore humming, "Night now,
to be on my way home."

Li Po

Looking Towards

Rock cedar trees and the glabrous leaved
ligustrum shrubs as egrets overflow
the mountain with white: above the chant
of the river rises stridor of apes.
But you can't face the Autumn Shoals,
like stone the sounds abrade the heart.

Li Po

I'll Write You If

Through the corkscrew hole of frontier
the men ride down autumn to gut our town.
Our soldiers come from homes;
no chess game. And all tallied up
we bed down on coiling sand.

The moon's bow jags its shadow
over this unentered stone gate,
and as frost pouts a flower on my blade
I dust and sigh it
to you.

Li Po

Good-bye to Cheng Shih Erh On Going To Meditation

To his house and garden patch at Kiukiang he climbs
to close out the world on the steep frontier.
And where mountain walls waive travellers,
last autumn's grass corrals his door.
Having done with the quick loom of the times
and sold all his herbs, his wordless goosefoot
staff pilots him upwards, past former sprouts
that the frost has fortified into joints
of bamboo. Facing him the mountain receives
the dieting sun. A stream irrigates
his yard as stray clouds befriend him. And the wild
mountain cinnamon now in bloom,
I'll go up and bring him a bouquet.

Liu Ch'ang-ch'ing

Meeting Snow Beneath

Anise leaf, illicium colors the mountain's
evening, without the gloss. Frost
grizzles white thatch of grass. Fire
wood stacks the door, and a dog barks at wind
sifting snow against a walking home man.

Liu Ch'ang-ch'ing

All Day The Hills Around The Shrine

Resonance night makes against edge
of house, a mist laminates into hammered flint
sound over trees, and pale whorls swag
the island wind in fronds of aquatic
plants. Now the dead leaves are storing frost
in the mountain and in the uncloudings of wild geese;
in the village someone pounds the moon's robe
on a washing stone. Facing the window
a pine draws the year's change
                              in my guitar's chords.

Liu Ts'ang

Snowfall River

江雪

The bird and mountain I can't get near.
Ten thousand walkings have eroded my footprints.
Only a lone boat, an old man beneath,
leaves on his shoulders and splint hat against rain,
fishes through the cold nap of water,
catching slow falling snowflakes.

Liu Tsung-yüan 柳宗元

千山鳥飛絕，
萬徑人蹤滅。
孤舟簑笠翁，
獨釣寒江雪。

The Fisherman

Under night in the narrows
a fisherman tied up his boat
along the craggy west cliff to sleep.
Then dawn hooped his pail
dipping up water from the Hsiang
as his bamboo fuel's spincs
sputtered to flame.
But his wisp of smoke melted
in the sun's upward plunging. And no
trace of him. Only undertone, "ao ai"
of oar-thole
caught in the widening trough
of river and joined stone.

Liu Tsung-yüan

Dawn, Going in the Valley

Layer on layer, frozen dew
droops twig ends. Then at daybreak
sallow leaves across the canyon bridge
to a tree-buried village, its wizened flowers
stare into frost clogged paths, and an underground
spring barely ties its thread of water. Make-
shifts of the mind I've been so long without, a great elk could range up now
out of the marsh,
unhurried, unhurried.

Liu Tsung-yüan

The Mounds, Early Spring Lifting

New warmth infusing this doorway:
about how many days would it take
to bring itself up along that wold
just above Ch'in, to snuggle close
around the village as if looking
for a place to snooze but in an old
plot of weeds, a working upward,
you'd hear a low murmur of thunder.

Liu Tsung-yüan

Wind Led

    Where
autumn homes
the wind's reach it
stays;
    stays.
Near the cold
it comes; brothers
date-line flight
of geese wing. It
    moves with-
out wait toward
dawn's stiff
house and
    tree. Man as
orphan first and
best hears it
on wide
    alone.

Liu Yü-hsi

Again

Sound slows at the falls;
drops down in the heard
voices rumouring the island's sweet underwood.

Foam throngs the upper bank's
enrolled flower buds.

Gradual sun sinks
footsteps; man to no
road. Social wasps, and baby swifts ambulate house eaves.

Lu Lun

The Waiting Lute

Above the watershed afternoon
grades the throat of the peaks as cloughs fall,
sudden sheep into shadow. Pine needles
weigh the moist night of moon while air
liquids wind talk. A woodcutter's legs
kindle to return past mist-nested birds,
and a girl's waiting is roof and door as an
unplucked lute in vine leaves
banks on its sound.

Meng Hao-jan

Not Finding Yuan

Went to Lo Yang to find a talented
man but he'd been exiled to the Sou
Mountains. It was O.K., he left word,
because the plums bud there earlier.

Meng Hao-jan

At Night Crossing The Hsiang River

A traveler counts his footsteps and waits
at the wharves where night has already made its
inning. And dew floats a pear tree's scent
on someone's lotus song around him. Then the oarsmen
push off, bearing toward a flame
on the far shore, past sleep-fathoming fishermen
inside a pale shell of mist; and voices
nearing in criss-crossing boats, the traveler
always asks, "Which way to Chen Yang?"

Meng Hao-jan

In Answer

Stubble overspreads the field east
and west, six, seven in
breadth li. My wood flute
plays three, four of the evening
wind's tones. Coming home
to enough food and yellow twi-
light, without slipping off
my grass rain cloak I
lie down in the bright
moon.

Mu Tung

In Reply to Ting Yüan-Chen

I doubt if the wind has moved spring around
sky's scarp since the second month doesn't bud
in these mountain thorps. Rotting snow
crams the limbs with oranges' weight
and the unthawed thunder is yanking up bamboo
sprouts. Night clamors with geese in the villagers'
dreams of planting as the raw earth year
is fraught with unfoldings. And you've already
incurred Lo Yang's downed flowers, but out here
the field grass sugars evening.

Ou-yang Hsiu

They Had Headed South But Then They Turned

The season's hard head lies in the year's
coffin. One brother east, another westward
are strapped to their getaway feet as a weed snarled
orchard field crops with shield and lance.
Highways' vagrant femur bones inch away
from their meat, and a bent bow in flight by his wings,
grief alone hangs in the miles of a wild goose.
This is nine autumns' heap of sprawl,
break down, thistle-drift. All see the same moon
through their own kind of tears, and at night your
heart beats awake in five different rooms.

Po Chü-i

Moored

Old tree trunk where shade
made smooth sloping the shore I tied my
reed-roofed bateau; and an angular cane helped
me eastward across the bridge; my
wrung out rain-soaked clothes would have watered the
flowering apricot blooms as the breeze in the
sun-blown willow lost its chill.

Seng Chih-an

The Gorges Of The Upper Yangtze

Witched peak beyond eye reach
convolutes downward, as out of mist
lithe parabolas joining
its own enigma, portend
with occult rain-pregnant caves,
the steep female shoulders.
  Moon washes white, intense as dawn
into three chasms and the nine affluent
streams walk upward on the spring tide,
as the gorges unfold up there
in her dream.

Shen Ch'üan-ch'i

Pear Blossoms

As a girl is thin
flame lipped east wind
caresses the door and
through grit-celled rainfall
the moon casts the hallway in
reverse. Too soundly. These dozing
anthers may hang down too far
in sleep. I light the candlewicks
to keep their make-up awake.

Su Shih

On The Fifteenth Night

Evening in doorways
step by step takes new leaf
in the stem of the day-blanched moon
where tree'd stars constellate lanterns.
And from south path a tied horse
near an east neighbor's girl in red slacks,
as meandering flute and string pluck
scent in a hidden window mesh.
Singing swarms the road
with wagon loads pressing
toward a threshing floor
to see who dances best.
And it never ends.
The tinging bell
lengthens the willow's
smooth limbs.

Su Wei-tao

Night At Cloud Gate Hall

By East Mountain the hall has charm.
Mist wreaths the parterres with elephant
teeth; and suspended lamps eye the night
with mountain spurs. Daybreak I unroll
the curtain as autumn unfolds the Five Lakes.
Nice. But I only remember one lonely
goose flight.
And that night the Tou and Nui stars made
a road from my window and earthed the sky.

Sun T'i

48

In Reply

Met on a pine tree's
floor comrade sleep
pillowing a high stone.
But a sunless almanac
buried in the mountain
awakened me shivering
wondering which year
it was.

T'ai Shang Yin Cho

Shed On The River

Paper screen, a square bamboo
bed's head rest. My
hand gone numb, dropped a
book into noon's
isothermal dream.
       Awake
felt at my lips
like sedge grass
a smile:
some fishermen out there
on the river, their
flutes playing tunes.

Ts'ai Ch'o

Going As Far As East Tower With Chang

Dark chains on the flat of dawn
as it damascenes the opening gates, and climbing
the wall stones to the coping the sun begins
grating the axles of coming home wagons;
and from the road's edge a willow bough bends
back and forth, sizing up each outsetting
traveler. Eastward, the road had smoothed its ruts
to the courier's tower and orchard; and clutching
petals embroider our coat sleeves
as a horse piebalds the horizon.
　　Then by a shop's stove, out-of-time Chi
wine, and not yet forenoon; silk
strings tied the pale stone crock, a wine
to the mouth like a breast as the fruit trees
buried our hoof marks by the river under white flowers.
　　Last night's barely heard rain clayed
inside calyces and the gold hangbirds
were still shaking out damp from their wings:
the letter from East Kuan always there
yawning on our drunk.
　　Once astride he twinged the reins,
and the horse spun away like a polished cane
spike. "When you coming back," I yelled.
"A hooked beaked bird heading east," he said,
"is no westward gyring swallow."

Ts'en Ts'an

Things At Fang Mountain

From a bridge in the orchard sunfall routes the winging of crows. And at
most through the limb-chafed air you can
make out two or three houses. The yard's
trees don't vacillate over someone
no longer here. Spring simply comes
back, and engineers old organs of plants.

Ts'en Ts'an

Letter Writing In The Dark

Dead leaf air crusts the boat-
landing's curb and swathes the voices
of calling people waiting to cross.
In a stand of trees a bell phrases
a shrine and lights begin to catch
at the river from a string of windows down
shore. Geese are drawing oblique lines; how
many villages stretch their wings? Now
the monkeys are treasuring their weeping,
and my isolated prow
boards a wordless moon.

Ts'en Ts'an

53

Dawn, Return To Mountain Hall

To the east trees sweat a milkstone
haze as cold stiffens wings edgeways. Birds steel
flight quills. Me too. Must go back up
Pe Mountain's grass slopes. The fifteenth
ends winter, offsets the moon to rendevous
with the sun, and impels empty paleas of old
grain; scaly light tricks out a stream's
weight of stacked away snow. And along
windrows they pile trashed mulberry
limbs to flame. Alone. Go. Fibrous
shadow will snake my feet. And wear
which clothes
under cold matted
overhang
of rain?

Ts'ui Shu

She Pounds Clothes

To know that war has no returns,
autumn kneels to rub clean the stone
as cold now nears the ear's bone from the moon's
gaze, unwrapping the long warp that waylaid
the heart: better to leave this pounding fatigue,
pack and send it all to the outer wall;
all I can and do I send from here
to you. I beat the stone. Listen. Listen!

Tu Fu

Dream of Li Po Going To Exile

Death gulps down the whole sound
of people. But leaving the living is two-sided
pain. And malaria will stagnate the ebb
and flow of your driven-to-bay news.

And tranquility is only panic's ghost
that gestures toward the border pass in endless
sycamores inking your haunted road.

But now you are seized in a bird net
as you try to flutter out of this winged dream.

As the timbers of the ceiling sink
in the moon I see your face
glittering like an engraved blade.
Watch out for the under-tow!
      Don't step on snakes!

Tu Fu

On Going To Frontier Duty

To draw a bow you have
to heave yourself into the nock.
To let fly an arrow, pull
back the whole arm's length.
To shoot a man, kill first
his horse; trick the rebels by first
snaring their chief.
Is there no way out
this closed door of dead men?
Just don't step across some
one else's
boundary
stones.

Tu Fu

Old Field

Twigs wattled between stakes,
as an old man interlaces a fence
for a dooryard where river ambage fans out;
fishermen drawing up their gill-seine
out of the T'an's flats, a trader's
sampan slips in on the pliable
rays of the anchoring
sun.
Traveling is an endless round
of crisis. Once you've crossed
the mountain passes called
The Double Edge and The Shelf
you are split.
A sliver of cloud for
a life. Can music glue
it? Our troops make no he-
roic returns in the east. And
from the walls of a lookout
a trumpet
hounds autumn.

Tu Fu

For Wei Pa, In Quiet

You're Orion, jagged, holothurian.
I'm Antares. We never meet.
But after twenty years my head
greys to the touch. It was dusk once, like this.

Chopped spring chives, new wine in cups.
The candle's power between our faces
recruits the old names on our heated breath,
and half our words sound like someone else,

a man brought to life, warmed over ghosts.
How many years of steps to your household
where your row of quick sprung children
buttonhole me with queries as they fill

urgent cups? Steamed yellow millet; ten
rounds; non-stop of wine, and still
not drunk. Only the night is. Only the
mountain is unsteadily dividing

now from all other tomorrows.

Tu Fu

The Night Of The Moon

The oblong moon binds all your pregnant
days around my imprisoned hands.
And your arms and cloudy hair emit
a fragile lightening above this political
orgy as we lean on this same sleazy
curtain of a thousand miles.

Tu Fu (in captivity)

In The Middle

Night harvests the clouds,
and sows the polished cold.
Straight up the silver stream
without sound
negotiates the moon's jade bowl.
This life, this night,
won't outlast the love of it.
Suspended
bright moon
next year
       somewhere?

Tu Mu

P.S. From Ts'ui Yung

Aggression's afoot in the army's big toe
as we are mobilized in the generalissimo's far
flung mind. And me the scribe of candid
keepsakes. Then the farewell feast waxes
from the river to the burg's twin lookouts
as our flags see-saw the wall's stones.
And since dawn the tigers and bears of our banners
have tracked the lunar wind until night
sleepily moaned in the guard's unfingered reed pipe.
And now I sit and stare at the mists
beginning to sidle through the camp with their brooms
against the day-raised dust. By now
the north wind has fleeced Ku-pe's streets.

Tu Shen-yen

Spring Dark

Incense burned out.
The stove's leak keeps up its drip.
The scissors of wind cuts, cuts,
and the cold repeats.
This spring I don't sleep.
And a calyx of shadow
further up the railing's shaft
migrates to the moon.

Wang An-shih

En Route

Slopes away
into glaze of distance
surplus wind shares in yellow mountain grass.
    My tied horse in metallic undersides
of leaves; suaveolens balsam
poplar I lean and think who
knows how infold these limbs
in a fulfilling; slippery grey bark then
fades, cracks, dwines.
    These firmed up family tombs
of Han face south toward
Changan's road and heart-rotted trunks.
Overhead flying squirrels spread
belly membranes to glide and fall
in old tree holes.
    Man's aftermath to scratch up jewels and jade?
Like sown grain man lives.

Wang Ch'ang-ling

64

Heard River, Foothills In Reed Tone

Then unlooked for
five plain stops of a flute
murmurs the river's moon
on planked wales pondering what course
holds. The sound along Chu Mountain
grooves, weaves, detours the barriers of Hu;
wanders one night-mind of a man
        by heart's rote
          uncombed river-hair ebbs under-
neath; unseen reach but known
                     echo-
piled trees deepen their drift
who know no family's boy but
Han-town nuance of tune but
strangers lifting oar blades to hide how
far empty enacts.
    Here stiff chill clots folded cloth on my chest.
Sharp bones of my horse; he keeps the road.
Driven to shift in exile
narrows speech why
white grass withers road's edge.
        Eight foot pole with cow tail
points me north toward diked walls
              through the night.

Wang Ch'ang-ling

Down North Ku Mountain

Who eats borrowed salt
will traipse the mountain's precinct
downward to find a hull
and stem nomad waves.
The two shores of the lake
separate like double doors
that never meet.
And wind-rise detrudes a sail down through the mist,
as the sea sun edges upwards
through the flaking away night;
and the Chiang swirled
where spring entered the old year.
A letter from home yes a
letter of home streets but to an
address I don't have.
A wild goose could leave it
on the outskirts of Lo Yang.

Wang Wan

Going Back To Sung Mountain

The stream's light bands this scrub wood
track making one the unceasing
beginnings of my wagon's horse path.
And birds rounding up evening in their
returns, tumble-down walls tend
old boat landings as the sun
empties its light in the steep combs
of autumn. If I don't make it
to Sung's foothills they'll
close the gates.

Wang Wei

By Wei Fields

Light kneels on the roof's pitch
as cows and sheep scramble up a scraggy
lane; and buoyed upon a staff in a hawthorn
yard an old guy foresees the boy
who grazes them. A pheasant crows
in the heading up wheat-sprouts and silkworms
sleep among the leftover mulberry
leaves. Men lugging hoes back from the fields
stand chatting, and never reach
an end.

Wang Wei

Mixed

A yesterday's village of the self
is always coming back to its streets;
a tomorrow's window to a plum
about to bear buds in the hoarfrost.

Wang Wei

For Chao Chien On Returning To Japan

The star's highwater mark you will
find through thick and thin to the east where
nine reefs swamp the void. Face dawn,
the one sure thing, candour bellying
your sails. But the soul of the world's
turtle will soar upward, blot the sun,
a cosmic frog. Fish will spurt their eyes
through the scarlet surf. And islanders will
hug you within an hibiscus, their
orphan host; but when you
get there how
will I know?

Wang Wei

Toward The Hsiang Shrine

None knows where the fragrant shrine lies
milestones inside the clouds' peaks
and beyond memory's roaded trees.
What bell voice could vault these cliffs
over the stone throat of the cataract?
But sun's color vitrifies blue spills of the fir
as evening on dragon feet
slithers in a pool.

Wang Wei

Wang Sun Driven To Hiding By The Soldiers Of An Lu-Shan

In the midst of the mountain farewells cease
as the sun's tail lurks by stacked wood and door;
then a year's green of spring leafs the light
and fate lines your shirt hem if you return.

Wang Wei

Letter To Li Ch'an

Last year
at the maturing of plants
you left.
Today, the sun
opens them
after a year.
What I've done
has come undone.
And the future lies
ghettoed
in its own
ingredients
as spring, an
opaque grief
sleepwalks through me.
Sickness clings to
my bones' dreams
of fields and farm folk.
And in this sinking land
money is ghost-ridden.
But there's word,
you on the way back
asking for me.
From the window
westward, the moon
is almost
full.

Wei Ying-wu

A Gift

At road mouth,
in sea arm and estuary, the long
lag of tide;
then deciduous days spend
blown leaves
strewing Tung Lake's basin.
Wine tastes night
fall; time to unmoor from Hwai Yin's
wharves as the rubbed
metal of the moon buffs a roof
over someone's singing.

Wen Ting-yün

74

Graffito

In the cold thatch
one clutch of lance grass
wind blown with thorns
to light the flame; whiff
warms the air and up.
Gone; leaves me cold.
To split some kindling sticks
for the stove, they catch,
groan-groan, flow, spread
slow genial heat.

Wu Ming Shih (anonymous)

When Then It Seemed

You were neatest. Leaning. Pitiable.
The problem I was became what you married
afterwards. You rummaged yellowed trunks to clothe
me. You plucked up gold hair pins by
the roots instead of eyebrows to fix my tricky wine
shakes. Sweet green weeds served at meals for meat;
leaf fall for kindling, we faced up to ghost locust trees.
And now I have this salary of ten
grand which I spend making a regular small
sacrifice. Its trickling liquid pours
again out on the ground
over your grave.

Yüan Chen

Your Bad News, Po

Maimed flame falls from its circle into a bleared
flag. Tonight heard your exile in Chiu-
chiang. I crawled to my feet and swayed
between your news and my guts' demise.
And black wind gasps through cold rain-teeth.

Yüan Chen

Biographical Notes

Chang Chi   8th and 9th cent. A native of Hsiang-chou in Hupeh. A scholar and poet who was patronized by Han Yü. A vigorous opponent of Buddhism and Taoism.

Chang Chiu-ling   673-740. Left 12 books. Tried to warn the Emperor Ming Huang about An Lu-shan but was banished. Later recalled. Used carrier-pigeons to communicate with relatives.

Chang Pi   In the Nan Tang or Five Dynasties period ca. 10th cent. Appointed as imperial censor. Left one book.

Chang-sun Tso-fu   794 Ca. T'ang. From Shuo-fang, in *Chung-Kuo Wen Hsüeh Chia Ta Tzhu-Tien.* 2 poems.

Chang Wei   From Honan, Ho-liang. At court of Tien Pao, 756-758, and Ta Li 766. One book of poems. Graduated as chin shih in 743. Vice President of Board of Rites.

Ch'ang Chien   8th cent. Short official career. Became a hermit devotee of Taoism, strong Buddhistic leanings. Ca. 749. Knew Wang Chang-ling. Graduated as chin shih 727.

Ch'en Tzu-ang   661-702. Wise official. Confucian school. Collected in ten books. Wild youth, finally began to study. Broke a costly guitar in passion over his own poetry. Died in prison.

Ch'eng Hao   1032-1085 Sung Dynasty. Published a valuable commentary on the *Book of Changes.* Scholar. Neo-Confucianist. Opposed Wang An-shih. Was tutor to Chu Hsi. Canonised in 1241.

Chu Fang   773 ca. Native of Hsiang-chou in Hupeh. Was

minor official. At the time of the court of Ta Li who came in 766. Left one book.

Ch'u Kuang-hsi   8th cent. From Jun-chou in Kiangsu. Graduated as chin shih in 726. Some 20 books. A censor about 750.

Fan Ch'eng-ta   1126-1193. Sung poet. Minister of state in 1179. Improved system of public labor and restored old irrigation works. Wrote on 35 varieties of chrysanthemums from his own garden.

Han Yü   768-824. Boldly wrote protests against extravagance of Emperor Hsien Tsung. Communicated with a crocodile. Delicate constitution, having studied assiduously as a child. One of the foremost in Chinese literature.

Ho Chih-chang   T'ang. 659-744. From Yüeh Chou. An official under Kai Yüan. He discovered the young Li Po. Drunk while riding, he fell into a dry well where he was found snoring.

Hsiang Szu   836 ca. From Chiang Tung. About the nien hao of Kai Ch'eng. Left one book. An official and scholar known for purity of his administration. T'ang.

Jung Yü   T'ang. Ca. 766. From Ching Nan. In the time of Emperor Ta Li. Left 5 books.

Kao Chü-ch'ing   A Sung dynasty poet.

Kao Shih   T'ang. Died about 765. From Ts'ang-Chou. About the time of Emperor Yung T'ai. Left 2 books. Suffered great poverty as a child. His songs and poems brought friendship of Li Po and Tu Fu. Travelled with an actress with whom he was in love, writing opera for her. After fifty began poetry and rivaled Ts'en Ts'an.

Li Ch'ang-fu   T'ang. Born ca. 876. As a Yü Shih official his imprudence won him banishment for life. Left one book.

Li Po   T'ang. 705-762. Perhaps China's greatest poet. Became the court favorite and then was banished, the victim of intrigue. Drowned embracing the reflection of a drunken moon. Widely travelled. Bold style, spontaneous. Taoist.

Liu Ch'ang-ch'ing   8th cent. T'ang. From Ho Chien. b.ca. 749 under Emperor T'ien Pao. A Master of Horse. 10 Vols.

Liu Ts'ang   T'ang. b.ca. 867 in Lu-Kuo. One book.

Liu Tsung-yüan   773-819. Famous T'ang poet, essayist, and calligraphist. From Ho Tung. Left some 40 vols. Involved in a conspiracy plot; banished for life. Knew well Han Yü who rebuked his leaning strongly toward Buddhism.

Liu Yü-hsi   772-842. From Chihli. Censor. Left 40 books. Lyric ability recognized by Po Chü-i. Banished to Yünnan. Great purity of idiom.

Lu Lun   8th cent. T'ang. Ca. 773. From Ho-Chung, about the time of Emperor T'ien Li. His poetry left in 10 vols.

Meng Hao-jan   689-740. From Hsiang-yang in Hupeh. Failed public examinations and lived as a recluse in the mountains. Became a great poet and was introduced to the emperor by Wang Wei. Admired also by Li Po and Chang Chiu-ling. Was inspired by riding a donkey over snow.

Mu Tung   The *Chien Chia Shih* says 'Nothing known.'

Ou-yang Hsiu   1007-1072. Sung. Neoclassical. Voluminous writer. Author of the earliest work on ancient inscriptions, history of the T'ang dynasty, an arcane work on the peony. Poverty as a child. Used Han Yü's paper basket for his writing paper. Fond of wine and company. Zealous for what he felt right.

Po Chü-i   772-846. Held a high office and then was banished to a petty post. Consoled himself building a retreat and writing poetry with 8 companions. Later held post of governor of 3 provinces. Left more than 2,600 poems engraved in stone. At seven months he knew many written ideograms. His daughter, Golden Bells, wrote good poetry at the age of ten.

Seng Chih-an   T'ang dynasty. Buddist priest, Ho Shang; Chih-an is a name in the Buddhist religion.

Shen Ch'üan-ch'i   T'ang. d.713. From Hsiang Chou. A friend of Sung Chih-wen. Left 10 vols.

Su Shih   Sung 1037-1101. Skillful in painting and calligraphy. Good in all the literary genres of the period. Political ups and downs. Exiled twice. His versatile talent in politics and his genial disposition enriched his poetry. Reigned supreme over the Tz'u poetry. Mixture of Confucian, Buddhist and Taoist concept of life. Always in trouble with those he ridiculed in his verse. In exile built a hut on an eastern hill slope.

Su Wei-tao   T'ang. 7th cent. 647-705. From Luan-chou in Chihli. Composed well at nine. Held high office. Left 20 books. Spent time in prison, then banished. Was known as 'Vacillator Su'.

Sun T'i   T'ang. d. ca. 761. From Wu Shui. About the time of Ruler Shang Yüan. An official, Repairer of Omissions. Followed style of Su Ting and Chang Chiu-ling. Some 30 books.

T'ai Shang Yin Cho   T'ang. No name known except the above nickname meaning The Great High Dark One. Lived, retired in Chung-nan in Shensi.

Ts'ai Ch'o   11th cent. Sung dynasty. From Chin-chiang. He was prime minister under Emperor Shen Tsung but was banished. Opposed Wang An-shih. In banishment he and his son, called Guitar, kept a parrot who would call out the boy's name. But the boy died, and the parrot continued to call the boy.

Ts'en Ts'an   T'ang. From Ho-nei. Held post of censor

under Emperor Su Tsung and Governor of Chia-chou. Left 10 books, 8 of which are in the *Ch'uan T'ang-shih* collection. Contributed to the reforms in prosody.

Ts'ui Shu   T'ang. b.ca. 749. About the time of T'ien Pao, Emperor. Was promoted to official post. Led rusticated life.

Tu Fu   T'ang. 712-770. Excelled in craftsmanship and technique. Realistic, humanitarian, family man. Suffered poverty. Master of regulated verse. Said his poetry would cure malaria. Wandered in the wilds of Ssuch'uan and had to live on roots for 10 days. Died from over-eating after rescue. Ranks with Li Po.

Tu Mu   T'ang. 803-852. From Lo-yang. Became a secretary in the Grand Council. A friend of Li Shang-yin. Called "Little Tu Fu." 20 books.

Tu Shen-yen   7th and 8th cent. From Hsiang-yang in Hupeh. Grandfather of Tu Fu. D.ca. 705. Friend of Su Wei-tao. Ten books. He got into trouble at a post in Lo-yang and would have been killed but his 13 year old son killed the attacker.

Wang An-shih   1021-1086 Sung. From Lin-ch'uan in Kiangsi. Great reformer, economist. New interpretation of the classics, included money payments instead of forced labor. Wanted candidates for the examination to be widely acquainted with practical subjects rather than style. He wore filthy clothes and did not wash his face. Omnivorous reader of medical and botanical books.

Wang Ch'ang-ling   8th cent. From Chiang-ning. D. ca. 756. Graduated as chin shih. Exiled to Lung-p'iao. Killed in An Lu-shan rebellion.

Wang Wan   T'ang. B.ca. 722. From Lo-yang. A friend of Chang Shuo.

Wang Wei   T'ang. 699-759. From T'ai-yüan in Shansi.

Graduated as chin shih in 721. Famous as a poet and a physician. Retired after being saved by the influence of his brother to being a poet surrounded by the joys of the country. Firm believer in religion of Buddha, never remarried after his wife died when he was 31. Turned his retreat into a Buddhist monastery after his mother died.

Wei Ying-wu   735-835. From Ch'ang-an in Shensi. Entered civil career after early life as body-guard of the Emperor Ming Huang. Became governor of Su-chou. 10 books. Lofty feelings, similar to T'ao Ch'ien.

Wen Ting-yün   B. ca. 859. T'ang. From Ping-chou. A friend of Li Shang-yin. Civil post. Was exiled. One book.

Wu Ming Shih   (anonymous)

Yüan Chen   779-831. From Ho-nan Fu. Composing at 9. Held an official post at 15. Friend of Po Chü-i. Rose to highest offices of State and died in disgrace and failure.

Appendix: Chinese Sources

Chang Chi	At Anchor Beneath the Bridge *CTS V, 1461. Lower side*
Chang Chiu-ling	At Black Mountain the Water Unrolls *CTS II,356. Upper side.*
	Touched Is Met *CTS II,348. Upper side.*
Chang Pi	Wind On Tung T'ing *CTS XIV,4385. Upper side.*
Chang-sun Tso-fu	Nan Chung Inn Before Rain *CTS IX,2831. Upper side.*
Chang Wei	The Lake, Eighth Month *CTS IV,1103. Upper side.*
Ch'ang Chien	At Anchor, Sunfall *CTS III,809. Lower side.*
Ch'en Tzu-ang	As Chiu Hua a Spring *CTS II,515. Lower side.*
	The Opposite Spring of Night *CTS II,513. Lower side.*
Ch'eng Hao	Hwai South *CCS 172*
Chu Fang	Its Bamboos *CTS VI,1869. Lower side.*
Ch'u Kuang-hsi	Staying Overnight on a Mountain Farm *Ku 23*
Fan Ch'eng-ta	Field's Family *CCS 163*
Han Yü	Small Rain *CTS VII,2037. Lower side.*

Ku refers to *Ku T'ang-shih Ho Chiai* (Ch'ung Ch'ing, 1968).
CTS refers to the *Ch'uan T'ang-shih* or *Complete T'ang Poetry* (Taipei, 1967) 16 volumes.
CCS refers to Ch'ien Chiai-shih

Ho Chih-chang	A Day's Other *CTS II,635. Upper side.*
Hsiang Szu	Overnight on the Mountain *CTS XI,3368. Lower side.*
Jung Yü	Wei's Place on the Han *CTS V,1606. Upper side.*
Kao Chü-ch'ing	Clear Easter *CCS 224*
Kao Shih	Cashiered *CTS IV,1206. Lower side.* Toward the Frontier *CTS IV,1207. Lower side.*
Li Ch'ang-fu	In Transit, Sobering *CTS XI,3620. Upper side.*
Li Po	War Wall South *CTS III, 923. Lower side.* It was Autumn *CTS III,945. Lower side. #1* Looking Towards *CTS 945. Lower side. #2* I'll Write You If *CTS III,933. Lower side.*
Liu Ch'ang-ch'ing	Good-bye to Cheng Shih Erh *CTS III,838. Upper side.* Meeting Snow Beneath *CTS III,819. Upper side.*
Liu Ts'ang	All Day the Hills Around the Shrine *CTS XI,3553. Lower side.*
Liu Tsung-yüan	Snowfall River *CTS VII,2083. Lower side. #2* The Fisherman *CTS VII,2087. Lower side.* Dawn, Going in the Valley *CTS VII,2083. Upper side. #1* The Mounds, Early Spring Lifting *CTS VII,2086. Upper side.*

	Letter Writing in the Dark
	CTS IV,1137. Lower side.
Ts'ui Shu	Dawn, Return to Mountain Hall
	CTS III,879. Lower side.
Tu Fu	She Pounds Clothes
	CTS V,1314. Lower side.
	Dream of Li Po Going to Exile
	CTS IV,1240. Upper side.
	On Going to Frontier Duty
	CTS IV,1241. Lower side.
	Old Field
	CTS V,1320. Upper left.
	For Wei Pa, in Quiet
	CTS IV,1222. Lower side.
	The Night of the Moon
	CTS IV,1304. Upper side.
Tu Mu	In the Middle
	CCS 177
Tu Shen-yen	P.S. From Ts'ui Yung
	CTS II,427. Upper side.
Wang An-shih	Spring Dark
	CCS 110
Wang Ch'ang-ling	En Route
	CTS III,789. Lower left.
	Heard River, Foothills in Reed Tone
	CTS III,795. Lower side.
Wang Wan	Down North Ku Mountain
	CTS III,648. Upper side.
Wang Wei	Going Back to Sung Mountain
	CTS III,702. Upper side.
	By Wei Fields
	CTS III,688. Upper side.
	Mixed
	CTS III,715. Upper side.
	For Chao Chien on Returning to Japan
	CTS III,708. Upper side.

88

Evelyn S. Field Library
Raritan Valley Community College
Route 28 & Lamington Road
North Branch, NJ 08876-1265